FAITH THAT MOVES MOUNTAINS

DEREK AMES

Self-published by Derek Ames through Gipping Press Ltd.

ISBN: 978-1-8381461-8-4

This is a non-fiction book.

The views expressed in this book are solely those of the author.

FAITH THAT MOVES MOUNTAINS

Scriptures quoted from the *Good News Bible* published by the

Bible Societies/Harper Collins Publishers Ltd., UK

American Bible Society, 1966, 1971, 1976, 1992.

Acknowledgements

I appreciate the hard work that Associate Priest Pauline Higham put in when proofreading the text and making suggestions for its improvement. This was a painstaking task.

I am grateful to Rev. Tim Hall for accepting the challenge to write the Foreword.

I am grateful to Jonathan Steed, (Director), and the staff at Gipping Press Ltd. for all their help and support to enable this book to be published.

I thank Apollo for taking some excellent photos in Uganda. He often seemed to be in the right place at the right time to capture some great shots.

A special thank you to Stella Davis for producing a spectacular design for the cover of the book.

Dedication

This book is dedicated to

Rev. Penry Hughes,

Rev. Daniel Cozens,

Rev. Peter Adams,

who demonstrated Jesus Christ to me
and inspired me to follow Him.

Rev. Penry Hughes   *Rev. Daniel Cozens*   *Rev. Peter Adams*

FOREWORD

Finally, brothers and sisters, rejoice! Strive for full restoration, encourage one another, be of one mind, live in peace. And the God of love and peace will be with you. 2 Cor.13:11 (New International Version)

Being asked to write a Foreword can be a very daunting proposition – but in this case it's an absolute pleasure.

I have known Derek for many years and it's a delight to read his story. This testimony of God at work in and through his life is a great encouragement – which is why the verse from Corinthians came to mind.

All of us who love and serve Jesus will find much here that is familiar - difficult decisions, terrifying steps of faith and uncertain futures. To read of someone who has shared all those experiences and emerged singing God's praises is an encouragement to us all to keep going!

Of course, the bit of the story I most relate to are the pages about Through Faith Missions; I've been working for and with them for 25 years now – its an extraordinary organisation that isn't terribly well known, but whose impact is immense. There aren't many places in the UK that haven't welcomed a Through Faith Missions team; and thousands of people have found that working with their teams has launched their own ministries. So it's no surprise, but a great joy to see how working on the Pennine Walk developed Derek's faith, skills and experience for his future ministry.

I hope and pray that as you read this you too will be encouraged in your walk of faith. And if you ever want to push yourself in that walk – well come and see us at Through Faith Missions!

May God continue to bless Derek in his extraordinary walk of faith and may you receive encouragement and blessing as you read this book.

Rev Tim Hall
CEO Through Faith Missions

Author Derek Ames

CONTENTS

	Page
Introduction	13
1. Invitation	21
2. What is Faith?	27
3. Through Faith	31
4. Reunion	41
5. Uganda	47
6. Uganda Again	53
7. Help!	63
8. Aid To Hospitals Worldwide	65
9. Tools With A Mission	67
10. Building Begins	71
11. Flying Solo	73
The Diary of Derek Ames on his trip to Uganda and Rwanda in March 2018	77
Tailpiece	99

Introduction

Have you ever wondered how God can make a difference in your life and in the lives of those around you?

"I alone know the plans I have for you, plans to bring you prosperity and not disaster, plans to bring about the future you hope for. Then you will call to me. You will come and pray to me, and I will answer you. You will seek me, and you will find me because you will seek me with all your heart." (Jeremiah 29: 11-13)

When we arrived in the Stowmarket area in November 1974, my wife, Pauline, and I, and our two daughters, Jenny and Liz, regularly worshipped at The Methodist Church in Stowmarket. We felt warmly welcomed into the fellowship and made lots of friends. Rev. Penry Hughes, the Minister, had a great teaching ministry and like a good shepherd, he encouraged his sheep to move forward in faith. He encouraged people to join prayer groups and house groups.

During the first few years when there was a Spring Bank Holiday week, he and Evelyn, his wife, organised a holiday conference, initially at Ashburnham Place in Sussex. He also encouraged people in the congregation to attend teaching sessions, including a day on healing with Rev. Trevor Dearing in Stowmarket and an evening on the Holy Spirit in Ipswich with Rev. Colin Urquhart.

When the first Monday in May became a Bank Holiday in the UK, appropriately on 1st May 1978, Penry took a coach load to Wesley House, Cambridge. In the morning there was worship and Bible study and after lunch participants were free to enjoy the sights of Cambridge.

Earlier that year two men from Bolsover Methodist Church in Derbyshire came to The Methodist Church, Stowmarket, to explain about Lay Witness Missions [1]. After the presentation, all those present were invited to vote by secret ballot for or against having a Lay Witness Mission. Penry, the Minister, was doubtful if there would be a majority in favour, but there was.

There were then six months till the Lay Witness Mission at the end of October. Every Monday evening there was a Prayer and Praise and Preparation meeting. On the final Monday before the weekend, when everyone was feeling inadequate and ill-prepared, someone started singing the chorus, 'Be still and know that I am God'. Everybody else joined in. From that point we had the assurance that God was in charge of everything and we must listen to Him. Towards the end of the week we were still in conversation with the Team Leader about whether there should be a young people's group or not, because of the few in regular attendance. By the end of the Mission this was probably one of the best aspects of the entire weekend.

During the weekend, as I heard our visitors give their testimonies [2], I realised they had all done something I hadn't, namely they had invited Jesus into their lives, or put in other words, they had surrendered their lives to Jesus Christ. After the Mission I spent more time reading my Bible and also reading two books that people had lent me, "My Father is the Gardener" and "When the Spirit Comes" both written by Rev. Colin Urquhart. I was also aware that many Christians were praying for me. In the weeks and months that followed I was drawn closer and closer to God. Up to that point the experiences Colin Urquhart [3] described in his books were outside my experience of what the Christian life was all about. I longed for God to bless me and fill me with His Holy Spirit. Sitting up in bed in the early hours of a morning in February 1979 I gave my life to Christ and asked Him to fill me with the Holy Spirit. I also asked Him to take me and use me for the extension of His Kingdom. There was no sound of angels singing, but I had the feeling I had made the right decision. It was only later that I realised it was God who had taken the initiative to draw me to Himself.

There was a greater sense of hope and commitment within the fellowship of The Methodist Church, Stowmarket, following the Lay Witness Mission. Monday nights continued as Prayer, Praise and Bible study. News of the Mission was passed on amongst Methodist Chapels in particular. On one occasion some of us travelled to the Chantry Estate in Ipswich and over a cup of coffee in someone's front room we spoke with folk from the local Methodist Church about what was involved in putting on a Lay Witness Mission weekend.

The next request came from the Minister at Peasenhall Methodist Chapel. We were given directions to the Chapel and I assumed this was easier to find than someone's house, because it was on the main road through the village. When we arrived we were ushered into the vestry and we realised this was going to be a different style of presentation to the last one. The Minister said we would have a hymn, prayer and reading and then he would hand over to us. Those who travelled with me from Stowmarket said that I knew more details about our Lay Witness Weekend, so I ought to start speaking and they would chip in as necessary! I hadn't previously been put into such a situation without any preparation. As I sang a hymn and listened to the prayer and reading, I wished the ground would open and swallow me up! I began to speak and as I heard my voice echoing around the Chapel, I realised they were not my words. Later I read Jesus' words to the disciples in Mark's Gospel, *"You yourselves must be on your guard. You will be arrested and taken to court. You will be beaten in the synagogues; you will stand before rulers and kings for my sake to tell them the Good News. But before the end comes, the gospel must be preached to all peoples. And when you are arrested and taken to court, do not worry beforehand about what you are going to say; when the time comes, say whatever is then given to you. For the words you speak will not be yours; they will come from the Holy Spirit" (Mark 13:9-11)*. OK, I was not standing before rulers and kings, but they were not my words; they came from the Holy Spirit. God had answered one of my prayers when I became a Christian, to share my faith with others.

Other changes quickly followed. A few days after my conversion, I met a lady from the Methodist Church, who asked me what had happened to me. I replied that a few days previously I had given my life to Christ. She replied, "It's written all over your face!"

It was as we considered what happened over the Lay Witness Weekend that I realised this had brought changes to the lives of various individuals, but these had Kingdom implications as well. Brenda, the Deputy-Head in an Infant/Junior School took early retirement and went off to train at Cliff College [4]. Two young people from The Methodist Church, Barry and Cath, also went to Cliff College to study and deepen their faith. Janet, a District Nurse, attended the events during the Lay Witness Weekend and was led to give up her job in the UK and offer herself for a six months placement with Tearfund [5]. She often wondered to which idyllic situation she would be sent. It turned out to be Somalia, not a peaceful haven as she had hoped. Her period of volunteering ended in November and Janet returned home in early December, when the shops were packed full of Christmas presents, food and drink. She had to take herself away on her own, because she just couldn't cope with the contrast between poverty-stricken Somalia and the extreme opulence in the UK. George and Brenda arrived in The Methodist Church in Stowmarket months before the Lay Witness Mission, which they looked forward to with eager expectation. Afterwards they believed that George should offer himself for the Methodist Ministry. He did so and went off for training at the end of the summer 1980.

As all these people stepped out in faith under the guidance of the Holy Spirit, they took on new work and responsibilities in the Kingdom of God. This introduction has described various ways in which people in a church setting have been called to move on in faith. At the end of each chapter there is something to think about on your own, or to discuss with others if you are using this book in a group.

1) What do you believe God is like? How would you describe faith?
2) Be still and let God speak to you. Close in prayer.

Footnotes

[1] A Lay Witness Mission involves a number of lay people from different parts of the UK spending a weekend speaking about their faith in Jesus under the direction of a team leader. The visitors are accommodated in the homes of people from the local church. At some point during the weekend each team member will say something about how he or she became involved with the Church and became a Christian.

[2] A Christian testimony tells about how a person became a Christian, and what has happened since. It is a person's story of faith.

[3] Experiences described by Rev. Colin Urquhart in 'When the Spirit Comes', in which he describes knowing he was a Son of God, and now filled with the Holy Spirit. In 'My Father is the Gardener', based on chapter fifteen of John's Gospel in the New Testament of the Bible, he paraphrases the words of Jesus saying that He is the true vine and Christians are the branches of that vine. Jesus goes on to say that we should remain united to Him, because a branch cannot bear fruit by itself, only if it remains in the vine.

[4] Cliff College is a Christian theological college in Calver, Derbyshire, in the Peak District National Park, with a particular focus on mission and evangelism.

[5] Tearfund is The Evangelical Alliance Relief Fund, a UK Christian relief and development agency passionate about ending poverty. It currently works in around fifty countries across the world, with a primary focus on supporting those in poverty and providing disaster relief for disadvantaged communities. It follows Jesus where the need is greatest, working through local churches to unlock people's potential.

1. Invitation

As time moved on, developments were taking place within The Methodist Church in Stowmarket and beyond. The numbers in membership at the church showed a steady increase year on year.

In March 1979 I was appointed Second Master at the secondary school in Debenham, with particular responsibility for helping with the development of Debenham Modern School into Debenham High School from September of that year. It was a friendly school with a hard-working staff. It had about 250 pupils, with that number expected to rise to over 400 within a few years.

Pauline, my wife, was asked to do the occasional supply teaching at Chilton Primary School, where our two daughters attended. Then she was appointed to cover a member of staff on maternity leave for the spring and summer terms in 1980, and then for the autumn term too. Subsequently she was offered a full-time contract at the school beginning January 1981.

Since becoming a Christian in 1979 I felt that someday I would take on a full-time Christian job in the Stowmarket area. I was uncertain what this might be, as about the only full-time posts were Vicars, Pastors and the like. I thought I would see a job advertised and then apply for the post and be appointed.

In the autumn of 1982, out of the blue, I received a phone call from Victor Jack, with whom I had a passing acquaintance and who had the reputation throughout East Anglia and beyond of being an excellent evangelist. Victor had been appointed as Chairman for the Mission England meetings to be held at Portman Road, Ipswich, in 1984, with Billy Graham as preacher. [1] Victor invited me to be Chairman for the Stowmarket Area churches in their preparation and follow-up for the Mission. I had only a few days to give him an answer. He told me I would have to appoint a team of workers, such as Treasurer, Prayer Secretary, Transport Coordinator, Youth Coordinator, etc. etc. I wasn't sure if I was the right person for this job. After all it was a Campaign being headed up by an American evangelist and I had never been to a Billy Graham rally. However, I reckoned if Mission England was aimed at preaching the Gospel and encouraging people to become Christians, it was something I had to be involved in. I felt this was a call from God and I had to step out in faith.

Pauline, my wife, said she would be willing to act as Treasurer. She felt she would be able to keep a careful eye on the finances and may not have to attend every Team meeting. I told her she could be the Treasurer only if it was the last post to be filled. A number of people were recommended to me by others and some rang me to offer themselves to serve on the Stowmarket Area Team. When I spoke to people on the phone for the first time, I would ask them what they believed their gifting was. The immediate response I received from the majority was to say that they didn't want to be Treasurer! When that post was the only vacancy that remained, I told Pauline the job was hers! I had never previously experienced such a clear indication from God for a particular person to take on a particular job. He had made it obvious that the person who volunteered originally was clearly His choice. No one else had come forward!

Everything about Mission England was well-organised and spectacular. There were some excellent preparatory events put on in Stowmarket and even larger ones in Ipswich. It was very special to be working with people from across the Christian denominations for the increase of God's Kingdom. The crusade meetings at Portman Road in Ipswich were memorable experiences, especially the large choir, guest performers and Billy Graham's preaching. Each evening large numbers filed down on to the pitch to surrender their lives to Jesus Christ and to be put in touch with local churches.

After the Crusade Meetings were over, many churches were just getting used to the experience and contacted the Stowmarket Team to ask what would be happening next. We were still meeting together on a regular basis, to assist churches with follow-up and we realised we must continue doing Mission. Our first idea was that we would plan an event for 1985, but this soon changed to 1986, when we considered all the work that would need to be done in preparation. Bishop Gavin Reid, who had been the overall Chairman for all the football ground missions with Billy Graham throughout the UK, still paid visits to Ipswich, to advise on follow-up and encourage ongoing mission. It was arranged that he would stop off on his way home, to meet with the Stowmarket Mission England Team and give some advice on possible ways forward. When he asked for the names of evangelists we had in mind to head up our mission, Rev. Daniel Cozens' name was put forward. Gavin Reid said he didn't want to hear any more names, because Daniel would do an excellent job. A number of us went to meet Daniel in the rectory at Coton near Cambridge. He told us about himself and his work as an evangelist and we and he agreed to go away and pray. Shortly after this we confirmed that the New Life Mission would be held in Stowmarket Regal Theatre and the nightclub opposite during the last two weeks in October 1986. Then we continued the task of making the Good News of Jesus known throughout the Stowmarket area. Some of the Stowmarket Mission England Team stepped down and others came in to take their places on the New Life Team.

1) Do you have a particular reading from the Bible through which God has spoken to you? How did God guide you using this passage of Scripture? How did you pray?
2) Pray about these matters, especially if some of them are awaiting fulfilment.

Footnote

[1] Mission England. After much prayerful preparation, it was decided that evangelistic preaching rallies would be held in various cities across the UK organised by The Billy Graham Evangelistic Association, with Billy Graham as the Evangelist. The meetings would be held in the spring and summer of 1984 in football grounds in Bristol, Sunderland, Norwich, Birmingham, Liverpool, and Ipswich.

2. What is Faith?

To have faith is to be sure of the things we hope for,
to be certain of the things we cannot see.

(Hebrews 11:1)

There were no signs of any jobs on the horizon. One
Sunday morning in June 1983 I took a service at the
United Reformed Church in Haughley, not far from
home. As I described in my sermon what it was like to
step out in faith, being like stepping off a cliff, but
knowing you would not die, I was quite overcome. I
remember thinking that none of the congregation showed
any signs of being affected, while I found it hard to hold
back the tears. Amazingly, I hadn't seen this coming
when I prepared the sermon a few days earlier. I couldn't
wait to get home to tell Pauline what had happened.

I realised it had to be a complete step of faith, not a small
one which I would only take when a job was given to
me. That would not be faith anyway. I would give in my
notice with nothing to go to. In July I wrote a letter to
resign from my post at Debenham High School,
indicating I would leave the school at the end of the
Autumn Term 1983. By this time I had already got
plenty to do in preparation for Mission England. Before I
left, Mr Arthur Holifield retired. He had been the only
Headteacher of Debenham Modern School and for the
first four years of the High School. He was replaced by

Mrs Angela McClelland. On the day she was appointed, I had to explain to her that the reason I would shortly be leaving had nothing to do with her appointment as the new Headteacher!

During the autumn I was led to read Matthew chapters five and six, seeking confirmation from God that I was following His prompting. *"Happy are those whose greatest desire is to do what God requires; God will satisfy them fully." (Matthew 5:6) "No one can be the slave of two masters; he will hate one and love the other; he will be loyal to one and despise the other. You cannot serve both God and money." (Matthew 6:24)*

"This is why I tell you not to be worried about the food and drink you need in order to stay alive, or the clothes for your body. After all, isn't life worth more than food? And isn't the body worth more than clothes? Look at the birds: they do not sow seeds, gather a harvest and put it in barns; yet your Father in heaven takes care of them! Aren't you worth much more than birds? Can any of you live a bit longer by worrying about it?" (Matthew 6:25-27)

"And why worry about clothes? Look how the wild flowers grow; they do not work or make clothes for themselves. But I tell you that not even King Solomon with all his wealth had clothes as beautiful as one of these flowers. It is God who clothes the wild grass – grass that is here today and gone tomorrow, burnt up in

the oven. Won't He be all the more sure to clothe you? How little faith you have!" (Matthew 6: 28 – 30)

I have never heard God speak as an audible voice. However, on a number of occasions I have had a clear indication of the direction I should take, such as when He indicated that I should resign from teaching. God makes lots of promises to us in His Word and the more we get to read them, the more we understand what He is trying to communicate to us. God promising to provide for the birds and flowers reminded me of His greater love for me with the words, "I will provide".

At this time Pauline and I thought we should warn Jenny and Liz that after I left teaching it was unlikely we would be able to afford luxuries like crisps and yoghurt. When we entered this period of greater hardship, we realised that his promise to provide was not just when money was plentiful, but when we had less. Several years later Jenny and Liz were talking about how many hundreds of thousands of pounds we as a family would have had if I had continued teaching. My response was always the same, "You tell me what you have gone without because I stopped teaching. You were able to have clothes as before and you went on trips, including visits to penfriends in France."

I was asked to do 0.5 of a timetable in a Middle School in the spring term 1984 and then I was asked to teach in a Primary School for the summer term 1994. Sometimes we would find half a dozen eggs on our doorstep. God knew our needs on these occasions and met them accordingly. My response was always to say, "Isn't God good!

1) Think about a time when God challenged you to step out in faith to serve Him. Did it feel like stepping off a cliff? How did things work out in the end?
2) Was there a time when you felt God was strangely silent? Pray to Him now.

3. Through Faith

When I felt that I should be doing some full-time
Christian work, I wrote to a number of organisations to
test the water. I contacted British Youth For Christ,
enquiring about the prospects of working for this
organisation. At that time I would have had to go away
to do a year's training and then be placed in a Centre
where there was a vacancy. As Pauline and I talked this
over, we thought this would make difficulties for the
family. Pauline had obtained a full-time teaching post
within recent years and both our girls had moved from
Primary School to Middle School. If I was going to be
away doing training for much of the year, we felt it
would destroy the firm foundation on which our family
had been built. In addition, if we eventually had to move
to another part of the country, the chances of Pauline
obtaining a teaching post and Jenny and Liz being placed
into a suitable High School would seem to be remote. At
that time Suffolk was different from most of the country,
having Primary, Middle and High Schools. At the time
we would probably have to move, Jenny and Liz would
have done two or three years at a Middle School and
would then have to start in the third year of a High
School. As it turned out Pauline completed 25 years
teaching at Chilton Primary School and Jenny and Liz
fitted very well into Stowupland High School. Jenny
went on to do a degree in French Studies and a Diploma
in Business Studies. The year Liz did GCSE exams there

was far more course work, which suited her fine. She went out to work after 'A' levels and has done clerical work ever since.

It was good to be involved with Rev. Daniel Cozens and his evangelical set up called Through Faith Missions (TFM). Much of the preparation for the New Life Mission was organised and delivered by Rev. Peter Adams, Daniel's assistant. A number of people from the Stowmarket area went on training courses for the New Life Mission and then volunteered to help with missions in other places. Each year there was a TFM Prayer Partners' Conference held in the premises of Holy Trinity Church, Brompton. These conferences were usually held in spring or early summer. I spent four years studying in Chelsea, but I had never taken the opportunity to look inside Brompton Oratory. On a particularly wet Saturday I took a few minutes off from lunch break at the Prayer Partners' Conference, to go and look inside the Oratory. Fortunately I had my coat pulled up to shelter my head from the rain. As I approached the door, it opened and a man inside asked the people in front of me "Bride or Groom?" I then beat a very hasty retreat! I still haven't been in Brompton Oratory!

After all the preparations for New Life, the mission fortnight finally arrived. We had a good team of people from various parts of the country to assist us. These had been team members who had worked with Daniel in other places. On one occasion we held a Men's Breakfast in a night club, with Daniel as speaker after we had eaten. I drove to the venue feeling something of a failure, because the two neighbours I had invited declined the invitation. Earlier that week, I had given a lady Local Preacher a lift to the Methodist Circuit Local Preachers' meeting. When I dropped her off at home, I gave her an invitation for her husband to attend the Men's Breakfast. He was not a regular worshipper and she said afterwards that he placed the invitation on the mantelpiece with other miscellaneous papers. His wife wasn't sure whether this was to remind him every time he saw it, or to hide it out of the way! When I arrived at the venue, he was the first person I saw and he willingly came and shook my hand. When Daniel had finished preaching and gave an appeal, this man was the first to respond and gave his life to Christ. O ye of little faith!

There were a number of converts throughout the fortnight of the mission and some others made a commitment at a later date. A number of these had connections with the Parish Church and two went into the Priesthood as Non-Stipendiary Ministers.

At about this time I was in contact with British Youth For Christ again and I was asked to meet with the East Anglia Regional Coordinator in Norwich. I then went for an interview at the YFC headquarters at Cleobury Place near Kidderminster. It was agreed I would start a YFC Centre in Stowmarket and gather a team around me to be involved with young people.

So what is faith? Trust, confidence, or belief. In the case of Christian faith it is trusting that Jesus died on the cross to forgive our sins and believe that He calls us forward to live for Him. Let me give some examples from the Bible:

"These (words) have been written that you may believe that Jesus is the Messiah, the Son of God, and that through your faith in him you may have life." [John 20:31]

"For the gospel reveals how God puts people right with Himself; it is through faith from beginning to end." [Romans 1:17]

"God puts people right through their faith in Jesus Christ." [Romans3:22]

"For our life is a matter of faith, not of sight." [2 Corinthians 5:7]

Each YFC Centre had a Chairman of its Management Team and each year these people would meet together for a weekend of worship, preaching, and prayer, and to report back on the developments during the previous year. It was suggested that I might join these Chairmen for their get-together at the end of the second week in February 1988. This would help me ease myself into the YFC family.

A few weeks previously my father had suffered a stroke and was admitted to hospital in North Walsham, Norfolk.

I visited him on the Thursday and as I left I shook hands and wished him 'God bless'. He had a puzzled look on his face as I left the ward. The next day I drove to Cleobury Place, arriving in time for the evening meal. We then assembled in the main hall and enjoyed a time of worship. It was during this time that I was handed a scrap of paper with my home telephone number on it and I was asked to ring my wife. She told me that my step-sister had just phoned to say that my father was dying and he would only last a few hours. Cleobury Place was more than four hours drive away from the hospital, so travelling there was not an option. I went outside and shed tears as I walked around the grounds. Again there was no actual voice, but the message was clear, "Your earthly father is dying, but I am your heavenly Father and I will take care of you."

My time with YFC was a blessed time and I was on a steep learning curve. On one occasion we had a morning's training in Norwich about doing street work, led by an experienced practitioner. Early on in the session we were asked what we feared most. Those of us who were rookies said things like, "Knowing what to say," or "How to engage someone in a conversation about God." The experienced street workers said, "Getting hit!" Some of us went out on the streets of Stowmarket on Saturday mornings and got into some good conversations. A number of us got involved in helping with youth groups and doing assemblies in schools. Each year we ran a Summer Camp under canvas at Sizewell Hall.

In discussion with YFC it was agreed to have a team of three coordinating the work of YFC in East Anglia, rather than a single Coordinator: Danny as an evangelist had headed up the Street Life Bus project for a number of years, visiting a number of locations during the evenings each week; Grantley was an evangelist who had been the sole Coordinator; I was asked to do the paperwork. One of the first things the three of us believed God had called us to do was to organise a Prayer Walk around East Anglia claiming it for the Lord. This took place during three weeks in May 1989 and involved full-time workers and trainees. The weather was fine and on the only day when there was rain a lady picked up the three currently walking and gave them shelter until the rain stopped. So even when it rained nobody got wet! Each night there was a Prayer Concert [1] with people from the local churches involved. After Saturday night's Prayer Concert we travelled home to spend Sunday with our families and then we resumed on Monday morning where we had left off on Saturday. On the last day we walked the Norwich Ring Road and concluded with an impromptu Prayer Concert in the Norwich YFC premises.

I was unable to attend the TFM Prayer Partners' Conference in 1989 because of the clash with the YFC Prayer Walk. Afterwards rumours circulated that Daniel

Cozens was thinking about doing a walk with men along the Pennine Way, as a means of doing evangelism. In November of that same year Daniel called a meeting to spell out what he had in mind. Churches within reach of the Pennine Way would be contacted and invited to put on a two-day programme, involving schools, pubs, streets, and churches on Sundays. It would take place over three weeks in May 1991. Men would be in teams of ten including the Leader and there would be ten teams looked after by a more experienced Centurion. All would sleep on church hall floors and rely on local congregations to provide food and drink. Every man would have to do a training weekend, which would include having a go at all aspects of the actual mission. It would be called the Walk of 1,000 Men. I decided if I was going as far as the Pennines I might as well go for all three weeks. I was appointed to lead a team for each of the weeks. When we stopped on the way to the opening service I can remember wondering what I was doing amongst so many vicars, youth workers and evangelists. I need not have been concerned, because God had everything planned. It was just like walking through the Acts of the Apostles [2]. I started at Hexham and the Walk ended in Edale. We didn't walk all that distance, often getting lifts by coach or car to our next destination. Many accounts have been written by many people about what God did during those three weeks and all the glory goes to Him. On the Sunday afternoon when two of us were doing door-to-door surveys for the first time on mission, we called at a house where a young lady aged 16-18 answered the door. Her parents came and looked over her shoulder, but encouraged her to do the survey on her own. She was certainly interested, but her answers didn't indicate she attended church. When we asked the final question, 'If you could meet God and ask Him a question, what would it be?' She replied, "What does God want me to do with my life?" And this was just the beginning!

Day after day God was at work in us and through us. There were so many God incidences. It didn't matter if you were doing door-to-door, chatting in a pub, taking a school assembly, preaching, or praying for someone to be healed, things happened. We didn't become complacent, because we knew this was the way God planned it. We always tried to make sure that none of the glory came to us, but that it all went to God.

I walked over 100 miles during the three weeks of the mission, carrying a rucsac that was far too heavy. Of the three teams I led, Team 28 holds the fondest memories. When we were on the local football pitch waiting to be allocated to the different churches, Team 28 was the team that got overlooked and was last to be placed. Christopher, the Vicar of the Parish Church, took us to his church and we bedded down in an upstairs room with carpet, where the crèche took place on Sundays. Another team was accommodated on the stone floor inside the tower. Throughout that week we gelled together so well, it was as if we had known each other for years. After the closing service at Todmorden at the end of the second week, we gathered together in a circle of prayer and I don't think there was a man who didn't shed tears!

1) If I asked you that same question from the survey sheet: If you could meet God and ask him a question, what would it be? What would you say?
2) If your life is very busy and hectic at the moment, write a prayer that you might say to God.

Footnotes

[1] A Prayer Concert often involves a time of worship and maybe a Christian speaker. However, the major ingredient is prayer. Sometimes this may be in groups, or an individual may lead the congregation, or maybe everybody prays together, all at the same time.

[2] The Acts of the Apostles is a book in the New Testament of the Bible. It describes what it was like in the early years of the Christian Church. There was much preaching going on and many people became Christians. It was an exciting time.

Rev. Charles with early arrivals for the opening of the Grace Memorial Day Care Clinic

The Grace Memorial Day Care Clinic

Start of new building to provide nurses' accommodation

Rev. Charles at the end of a busy day

Immigration buildings on the Uganda side of the border

Derek standing in Uganda with Kenya behind him

Doctor Stephen, Derek, Rev. Charles and Charles' daughter Jane

Jane making sure Derek didn't get lost

Jane, Derek, Rev. Charles and Doctor Stephen at the border

Doctor Stephen, Derek and Jane stop for drinks in Kenya

Derek and Doctor Stephen in Kenya

A little boy hiding among the clothes

One of many mopeds

Headteacher (in orange top) with Derek and Jane
outside Bumbo Secondary School

Setting off on a tour of the school

Classroom

Classroom block from the outside

Queue for lunch

Science block

Derek and Jane in front of mission and core values at Bumbo High School

4. Reunion

Many incredible stories emerged while the Pennine Walk was taking place and after it had finished. Perhaps men had more time when they got home to write down what happened and to consider the implications of what had taken place. Already churches from Cornwall had got together to invite Rev. Daniel Cozens to lead teams throughout Cornwall in 1993.

After all that team 28 had experienced on the Pennine Walk, there was a strong feeling that we should get together as soon as possible to continue doing evangelism. Eventually we agreed on a weekend in October 1991, based at Bedford Baptist Church, with wives invited too. I have very little recollection about what happened on the Saturday, apart from trying to speak to people in a very crowded pub that night.

At the Sunday morning service Rev. Steve Chalke was the speaker and he challenged people as they left. This was not long after the Berlin Wall came down and the Soviet Union had splintered into separate pieces, the largest of which was Russia. Steve Chalke asked me if I had been to a Third World Country and when I said I hadn't, he said, "Get out there; there's so much you can get involved in." Arthur and Paula, who lived not far from Stowmarket, had taken a number of family holidays inYugoslavia each August prior to the changes taking place. They decided to continue travelling to Yugoslavia each August, taking with them a lorry laden with food, clothes and toiletries. Over the years, others joined them and they were able to take more lorries laden with goods. I thought perhaps I might volunteer to join them in reaching out to this part of the Third World.

As the Youth for Christ group in Stowmarket grew, we were able to have a number of trainee evangelists from British Youth for Christ working with us. I was also involved in work with Bryan setting up an outreach group, called Target Youth, in North East Essex. This project originated from the local churches under Bryan's guidance. It also took on evangelists and later offered trainee evangelists from British Youth for Christ a one year placement.

Because of my involvement with several of the churches in and around Stowmarket, I was invited to join the Ministers' Fraternal at their occasional meetings. Having had a close working relationship with the Parish Church of St. Peter's and St. Mary's in Stowmarket and because of it taking on trainee evangelists, I felt led to move to that church in 1994.

At the time I moved, Jeremy, the Vicar, asked me if I would be interested in training as a Reader, but at that time I declined and said I just wanted to be part of a worshipping community. Later he asked me again, saying that he was getting near to retirement and his replacement might 'go by the book' and only those with a licence would be allowed to preach. I agreed for him to find out what extra training I would have to do, bearing in mind I had trained as a Methodist Local Preacher some years previously. It was agreed I would have to complete Year 3 and some parts of Years 1 and 2. I also joined an excellent study group led by Rev. Christine. I still meet some of the members of that group from time to time.

There was in St. Peter's and St. Mary's Parish Church in Stowmarket a Church Army evangelist called Don. Whilst at Church Army College, he and his friend, Kerry, agreed to do missions in each other's parish on a regular basis after they left college. Kerry lived in Hemingford Grey, near Cambridge, not far along the A14 from Stowmarket. So in the autumn of 1994 a mixed group of ordinary people from Stowmarket went to do a mission in Hemingford Grey, consisting of lots of door-to-door surveys and some evening events. I remember the mission for two reasons: 1. I had accommodation in the Archdeacon's house, which had a large window at the top of the stairs depicting Ugandan cranes, the emblem of Uganda. 2. There I met Charles Mugisha, who was amazed to see his country's emblem displayed for all to see in the house where he was staying! Charles was a fiery preacher and kept saying to those on the mission team, "You must come to Uganda." Don and Kerry took up the challenge in 1995 and went on a fact-finding trip with a view to taking a team to Uganda in the near future. 1994 was the year of the

Rwandan Genocide, so they were able to go on to Rwanda and visit some of the Genocide sites. Don and Kerry also had opportunities to preach peace and reconciliation to many prisoners, who had been arrested as being instigators of the Genocide.

Over the weeks and months that followed Don and Kerry investigated the possibility of closer links with Uganda and Rwanda. Child Sponsorship schemes were set up; a House of Mercy for ex-prostitutes was built and schools were established. Don set up RSVP[1], to encourage people in and around Stowmarket to reply and donate money to set up a charity to finance the various projects. Kerry set up Signpost as a separate charity, but run along the same lines and with similar aims to RSVP. They also planned to lead a trip for young people to Uganda in the summer of 1996, to enable them to experience Third World culture. It was to be based in Gabba, a community not far from Kampala, with a church that met in a large marquee, where Charles Mugisha was Pastor. In the event the trip attracted thirty mainly older people. Orientation days were held to acquaint us with what to expect. This was the time of developing new technologies in the UK, but not in Africa. Various members of the team managed to persuade individuals and businesses to donate computers that were to be taken to Uganda and given to Gabba Primary School.

1) Have you ever been to a Third World Country? What was your impression of it?

What did you learn from your experience?

2)   Pray about how you could be involved in a Third World country in the future.

Footnote

[1] RSVP is an abbreviation for respondez s'il vous plait, which means please reply. This is God calling us to reply to social issues like homelessness, drought and famine, as people become involved in eradicating these human miseries.

5. Uganda

On the Sunday before we travelled to Uganda, the Ministry Team at St. Peter's and St. Mary's Church in Stowmarket prayed for those of us going to Africa. As she prayed, Carol gave me a reading from Isaiah. "I don't know what it says, but I believe it's relevant,." She said.

"The Lord says, 'Here is my servant, whom I strengthen – the one I have chosen, with whom I am pleased. I have filled him with my Spirit, and he will bring justice to every nation. He will not shout or raise his voice or make loud speeches in the streets. He will not break off a bent reed or put out a flickering lamp. He will bring lasting justice to all. He will not lose hope or courage; he will establish justice on the earth. Distant lands eagerly wait for his teaching." (Isaiah 42:1-4)

This is a prophecy about the coming Messiah and the last line seemed to be particularly appropriate for me as a teacher. The thirty of us had been divided into three groups: one for pastoral visiting, one for evangelism, and one for teaching about computers. I was in the evangelism group and I expected to do quite a bit of preaching.

As we gathered at Don's house waiting for the coach, I took the opportunity to ask Don what we would actually be doing when we got to Uganda. He replied, "If someone says, 'Get on the coach,' get on the coach! If someone says, 'Pray,' then pray! If someone says, 'Stand up and preach,' stand up and preach!"

We had a night flight from Heathrow to Entebbe. There were quite a few people at home who were praying for us. The results of their prayers were experienced as we checked in at Heathrow. There were a number of trolleys laden with computers and accompanying equipment. All this passed through customs with no problems and without any tax being charged.

Landing at Entebbe is quite an experience, particularly if you you've not done it before! The plane comes in over Lake Victoria and you just hope there is a runway somewhere on which it can land!

When we assembled at Gabba Primary School, Nathan, the Headteacher, asked those who were teachers to put up their hands. Five of us did so. Nathan told us he wanted us to take classes, while his teachers learned how to use computers. So that was it! The last line of Isaiah 42:1-4, *"Distant lands eagerly wait for his teaching,"* referred to actual teaching! I spent every morning of the first week teaching Maths and English to classes of over fifty. It was a lovely experience because the children were so eager to learn. At the end of each lesson I told them something about England and invited them to ask questions. Over twenty years have elapsed since that first visit to Uganda and I'm sure that standards in Uganda Primary Education have improved beyond recognition.

There were trips out from Gabba to a number of places. Jinja had the appearance of a colonial city. We visited the Source of the Nile and there we saw lots of birds of many different colours. It was a wonderful spectacle. We also went to the Bujagali Falls, where youths would throw themselves into the cascading water, clutching only a plastic jerry can, for very little money! There were masses of water hyacinth growing in parts of the River Nile and this caused great problems for boats and ships that use the river, and for hydroelectric power stations.

The Sunday service at Gabba Community Church was a new experience: there was a warm welcome; lively music; powerful preaching by Don or Kerry, interpreted by Charles or one of the other local pastors; and an opportunity for some of us visitors to give testimony. There was also time for people to move around within the marquee and chat to others. I was accosted by a couple of teenage girls, who wanted to know if I was saved and was I sure! I met an older man with white hair who was clutching a Bible. He told me, "We not only read this book, but we live by it!"

One evening the local ladies cooked for us a chicken meal made from chickens which roamed around the houses. We reciprocated by cooking fish and chips. After this we entertained our hosts by singing well-known

English songs such as "London's Burning!" After the local ladies had fed us they did some Ugandan dances. They tried to get the British men to join in. We came to realise that Ugandan women are able to wiggle their hips in a way that British men can't!

One morning a small group of us did some pastoral visiting. One of the Ugandan pastors interpreted for us. One particular visit spoke volumes to me. A lady carrying her baby welcomed us to her home, consisting of two rooms with a curtain between them. We had to sit outside because there was insufficient room inside. She told us that her husband was a businessman. I found it difficult to imagine a man in a suit emerging from this house each morning and then travelling to work. The lady explained that every morning he went to the market and returned with bags of charcoal, which he would tip in front of the house. He would then sell this to neighbours and he would make a very small profit. As our visit came to an end, the lady came round and washed our hands and then gave each of us a small banana. My eyes filled with tears. For someone who had so little, she gave from the little she had to bless us. It reminded me of the widow in Luke chapter 21:1-4, who gave to God all she had. I believe the Lord approved of what the Ugandan lady did.

We spent a few days in a National Park before we returned home. We were told that there was more chance that the food served in the restaurant would be OK to eat.

Not true! The only place I picked up an intestinal bug was in the National Park! A quick dose of medicine and going without a meal soon dealt with the problem and the next day I was back to normal. The only excitement I missed was a hippopotamus scattering flower pots on the terrace!

There were many friendships between Ugandans and British that began with this trip. Child sponsorship schemes were set up by RSVP and Signpost. There were exchanges by music groups and evangelists. The stage was set for further developments in the future.

1) Read the story of the Widow's offering in Luke Chapter 21:1-4 and compare it with the Ugandan woman giving out bananas to rich Christian visitors? Listen to God and pray about what you could do to help poor people.

6. Uganda Again

Don wanted to return to Uganda as soon as possible and take Adam with him, to capture photos that could be used in RSVP magazines and publicity leaflets.

I also wanted to go back, to meet some of the people I had met on my previous visit.

Stephen, a teacher at Gabba Primary School, told me to ask Don to arrange a mission in his home parish of Bukimwanga. He had talked it over with his Archdeacon, Arphaxad, who was very pleased with the suggestion. The music for the mission would be provided by the band from Gabba Community Church. The trip was planned for sometime in May 1998.

Don wanted to develop projects in Rwanda and so he arranged for three of us to fly from Gatwick to Entebbe and then for he and Adam to immediately fly on to Kigali, where they would work for the first week. I would stay in Gabba that week, having accommodation with Pastor Peter, and Irene, his wife. Nathan was no longer Headteacher at the Primary School, but he was there to meet me on the first morning. It was arranged with the new Headteacher that I would teach each morning in the Primary School. Nathan said he would like to take me out to places of interest during the afternoons.

On Monday afternoon we caught a taxi to Kampala, so I could post a letter. As we neared the city there were people carrying placards and pieces of trees and bushes, to demonstrate support for the Mayor of Kampala elected the previous day. When the successful candidate had put up for election, he said he was supporting the poor and those of the lower class. This obviously gained him a big following across the city, but there were questions asked about him not having all the qualifications needed to be a candidate. A few days after he was elected, it was discovered he had not passed an 'A' level, so he was removed from office! There was turmoil in the city as people left work early and tried to get a taxi home. Nathan grabbed my hand and rushed me to the Post Office. Then we managed to get a taxi back to Gabba. As we were nearly there, Nathan said to me, "I was scared when we were in Kampala!" I replied, "So was I!" Nathan rang me that night, to say we would go to Entebbe the next afternoon to visit the gardens of a hotel, where the monkeys are afraid of black people but not afraid of white people. I asked if it was wise to go through Kampala after today's experience. Nathan said, "There will be no problem. Tonight the police and army will move in and disperse all the demonstrators and tidy up the streets. He was right. There were no signs of the previous day's demonstrations. In Kampala we caught another taxi to Entebbe, but it started to rain when we got there. We got lifts on two mopeds and the riders gave us umbrellas to keep riders and passengers dry. We must have looked very comical! Nathan and I were unable to keep the riders dry because the rutted roads made it impossible to keep the mopeds on an even keel. At times the umbrellas completely obscured the riders' vision! We eventually made it to the hotel as a storm broke. We had to stay under cover until the storm passed away and when it did, all the lawns were flooded. We made our way back to Kampala and then on to Gabba, without seeing the monkeys!

Each morning I would catch a taxi to travel to Gabba Primary School. One morning before I was due to leave, there was a very heavy thunderstorm and the roads were awash. I had been told what to do when the weather was unfavourable – don't travel to school until the weather has improved. There was a problem in that I was to do the devotions for teachers in the staff room before school began. I met the Headteacher when I arrived and he said I could do the devotions at the start of the lunch break. As I finished the lesson before lunch and started to make my way towards the staff room, there was the sound of beautiful harmonies filling the air. It was a lovely introduction to me leading the devotions.

Saturday was a busy day. The worship band from Gabba led the worship at a Scripture Union study day held at The King's International School in Kampala. I went along with the band. After worship we had to put all the instruments back in the bus (it would be called a coach in the UK) and take them to Gabba Church. Then the bus had to collect wives and children to go to Millie's wedding. I met Millie as a teacher in Gabba Primary School two years previously. Because of the number of things we had to pack in that morning we arrived late. Some said they wouldn't go into the ceremony, but I wanted to go in to experience a wedding Uganda-style. When some of the officials saw a white man (Musungu) come in, I was shown to the front, so I got a good view of what was going on. There was a small group of men and women on the other side of the church and I wondered what part they would play. During the signing of the register this group sang beautifully unaccompanied. After the wedding we all got back on the bus and went to the reception. This was a grand celebration. When it was all over we crowded together on the bus. It really was a squash! Peter asked me what I thought of travelling like this and I said, "It's OK!" Peter replied, "This is Africa!"

I had to preach in a church some distance from Gabba on Sunday morning. Nathan said he would let me have the travel arrangements. By the time we arrived at Pastor Peter's house on Saturday the electricity had gone off, but I managed to find a note that had been pushed through the door. We caught a taxi and then walked the rest of the way to the church. After the service we walked to the pastor's home for lunch. The pastor explained that it was customary to pick up the beans, matoke (mashed banana) and rice with the fingers, but he had provided a spoon for me. Four of us sat down to eat, the pastor and a man from the church, Nathan and I. No ladies sat down with us.

After lunch we went for a stroll, firstly to visit a lady from the church who was sick – this usually means suffering from malaria. She was most grateful to have a white man pray for her. After that we continued to stroll and if we met someone the other men knew, we would stop and talk. Then we would walk on. When the light started to fade Nathan said it was time to catch a taxi, which took me back to Gabba.

When Don and Adam came back from Rwanda, Don spoke at a lunchtime meeting at the World Trumpet Centre [1]. The format is always the same: visitors get a warm welcome and are shown to the room at the back. Ugandans are very mindful of British visitors and they provide them with bottles of Fanta to ensure they do not get dehydrated. After some prayers, we got shown to the seats at the front of the sanctuary. I had previously told Don of a song, 'Lord I come to you', that had been going round my head since I woke up. I wanted it to be played after I had spoken. Don said he wasn't sure they would know it, as it was a relatively new song. He said that while I was speaking, he would have a word with the worship leader and ask if we could sing that song when I finished speaking, but today it was a lady leading worship! As we sat there and one song ended, the lady changed the tempo and the band played the introduction to 'Lord, I come to you'! I looked at Don and he indicated that he hadn't said a word to the worship leader! God showed that he was not only there with me, but there ahead of me!

The next two days were spent packing things to go to Mbale and on to Bukimwanga! Before we left England the three of us were concerned about stories in the news that the Karamojong were killing people and stealing their cattle in the area to which we were about to go. Don asked Pastor Charles about this and he said we didn't need to worry. "We have no cattle, so we will be safe", he said.

We travelled in the bus to Mbale, with some of the church band taking instruments to lead worship. We met Archdeacon Arphaxad Namonyo in Mbale, who took us on a tour of St. Andrew's Cathedral. We then visited the Bishop to let him know the plans for the mission in Bukimwanga. He was not involved in the mission and was pleased his Archdeacon was in charge of the arrangements.

Arphaxad told me his name goes back to the book of Genesis chapter 10, being a descendent of a son of Noah after the Flood. It was also at Mbale that I first met Rev. Charles Mella, who was part of the Cathedral staff. The link with Charles would go on through letters and emails for over twenty years.

In April, Stephen Masiga sent me an email saying that all the plans for the mission in Bukimwanga were in place and wishing us a good time, but he wouldn't be there! He left for the United States later that month to work for a church in Chicago. For someone who had never previously left Uganda, this was a bold move. He has been there ever since!

Each morning during the mission there was worship and teaching in the church and in the evening (in the UK it would be called afternoon) there was worship and an evangelistic address by Don or Pastor Charles.

There was a tall Ugandan who wore shorts and everybody referred to as the doctor. We never did find out whether he was a real doctor or whether it was a name he had been given. When he found out that I was fifty-five, which is old by Ugandan reckoning, he offered to provide me with a walking stick! I thanked him and said I could manage without.

It was arranged that on Sunday morning I would preach at a small settlement, about five miles away. It was pointed out to me by some of the Ugandans, but they told me I wouldn't be able to walk there, because it would make me exhausted and dehydrated. Someone gave me a lift in a four track vehicle. I found out that some of the people I had already met were step brothers and some step sisters came from other parts of Uganda and also from Kenya. Such was the importance they attached to gathering as a family to meet this white preacher. I thanked them all for being there. Charles gave me advice before I set off on my preaching expedition, to only drink bottled water, to only eat food that had been cooked thoroughly and only eat fruit which had an outer skin.

There were some spectacular African red sunsets while we were in Bukimwanga. On the final night there was a thunderstorm and torrential rain, so even the main tracks became mud baths. A bridge that spanned a small river had rotted away over the years, but if the bus could negotiate the crossing, it would save considerably in distance and time. The driver tried revving the engine, but the bus sank deeper into the mud. After a time all the passengers had to get off the bus, but still it refused to budge. Don did an impression of Alan Whicker, saying we were marooned in the heart of Africa and we were due to fly home the next day. Eventually a local farmer brought his tractor and attached it with chains to the bus. Inch by inch it was pulled free, amidst great celebrations from visitors and locals alike.

1) Describe a situation in which you became trapped and there seemed no way out.
   What did you do and what happened? How was God involved in your rescue?
2) Pray for people trapped by drought, famine, floods, or family issues.

Footnote

[1] The World Trumpet Centre is the name of a church in the centre of Kampala. Many people who work in Kampala come to the church at lunchtime to join in worship and prayer and hear a Christian speaker.

7. Help!

Rev. Charles Mella wasted no time in telling me about the poor state of health of the people living in Uganda. Communicable diseases such as malaria, HIV/Aids, and TB were responsible for the greatest number of deaths in the country. However heart disease and high blood pressure were all too common and many people suffered from diabetes and diarrhoea. At that time I was unaware of the problems caused by circulatory diseases, let alone what caused them. Rev. Charles told me there was no state pension in Uganda and this didn't surprise me. Neither was there any clergy pension, which was not unexpected. Very often when clergy retired from ministry, they were left to their own devices and some resorted to begging on the streets. Charles set up regular meetings for clergy when they retired, to enable them to continue to enjoy fellowship. He also ran classes on keeping chickens and pigs to generate an income.

Charles suggested the idea of opening a shop in the area in which he lived, to provide medicines to help alleviate some of the common diseases. Charles' wife, Grace, was involved in serving in the shop. Then, out of the blue, Grace died, which was a bitter pill for Charles, his family and the whole community to swallow. Charles had to re-think the project, especially as the idea of enlarging the shop was no longer a possibility. The local council wanted to divert a road, to go through where the shop stood! One thing was clear in Charles' mind; the new building would be built as a memorial to Grace, his late wife. There were many discussions and planning decisions to be made, but eventually permission was granted for a facility to be built to help improve the health of the people living in the area and it would be called The Grace Memorial Day Care Clinic.

1) Describe an event that took place in your life, when everything seemed to go wrong. What happened? Who helped you?
2) Pray for someone experiencing difficulty at the moment.

8. Aid To Hospitals Worldwide

In the early stages of the project, I was uncertain of the types of equipment that Charles would need. Somebody suggested I contact Aid To Hospitals Worldwide (A2HW).

Mike Coleman happened to be at West Suffolk Hospital one day when he saw a driver loading a large piece of equipment on to the back of his lorry. Mike was intrigued and went and had a word with him. The piece of equipment was an X-ray machine, which Mike assumed was being taken away for repair, but the driver told Mike it was being scrapped! This alarmed Mike and on making enquiries, he found out that equipment worth thousands of pounds was being scrapped from hospitals in the UK every week.

Mike contacted a number of people about this situation and in December 2006 the charity Aid To Hospitals Worldwide was set up based in Bury St. Edmunds, with Mike Coleman as CEO. Collections were made from hospitals throughout the UK of used or redundant hospital equipment and these were taken to Bury St. Edmunds. Here the equipment was repaired or serviced and catalogued before being made available to charities working with hospitals overseas. Alongside the engineers and drivers there was an equally efficient clerical team working for Aid To Hospitals Worldwide directed by Jackie Keens.

After consulting Rev. Charles Mella and Jackie Keens, I was able to put together a list of equipment to be sent to Uganda. Although all items were free of charge, money had to be paid for transport from Bury St. Edmunds to the place where the equipment would be loaded into a container (around £100) and then there was the cost of shipping the container to Uganda. This amounted to £2,500 to buy the volume required in the container to transport the hospital equipment to Africa.

1) Describe an experience you have had, similar to Mike Coleman at West Suffolk Hospital. Was there a good outcome, or did things carry on as before?
2) Prayerfully consider how you could get involved in helping poor people, as Christians have done down the centuries.

9. Tools With A Mission (TWAM)

Over forty years ago the Baptist Men's Society asked Jack Norwood to head up a project making incubators. The next request was for solar powered incubators and Jack went out to Zaire (now the Democratic Republic of the Congo) for a year to develop them. John Bennett, a teacher, became interested in the project and this was the start of Tools with a Mission. John came to realise the need for tools in Zaire and he encouraged pupils in his school to collect agricultural tools and clean, renovate and paint them to go to Zaire. A sponsored event raised money to ship the tools and this was the first Tools with a Mission shipment, sent to a missionary working in Zaire.

John realised there must be many people like the missionary in Zaire, who were trying to teach people how to use tools, but without having many actual tools. John suggested the collection, cleaning and refurbishment of unwanted tools to the Baptist Men's Movement and so Tools with a Mission was launched in 1984.

At first a double garage was used as a base for refurbishing tools, then a barn and later a large warehouse. First of all work was carried out monthly, then weekly and eventually daily. With a huge increase in work, space was at a premium, in spite of adding two 20-foot containers and a Portakabin for the office staff. In 1999 Tools with a Mission was registered as a charity supported by most Christian denominations and many secular organisations. There are now collection centres and refurbishment centres across the UK, but Ipswich is the hub of operations. This necessitated movement into a larger warehouse on an Ipswich industrial estate. From here containers have been sent out over many years on behalf of Don's charity RSVP and it was here that I watched a container being filled with medical items to go to the Grace Memorial Day Care Clinic in Uganda.

Over recent years there has been an emphasis on providing training in a wide variety of disciplines and when trainees graduate they are presented with a kit to enable them to set up a business. The following were sent out in 2018: Carpentry kits, Builders kits, Groundworkers kits, Agriculture hand tools kits, Garage kits, Plumbers kits, Electricians kits, Garage mechanics kits, Hand knitting kits, Sewing kits and many more. In 2019 TWAM sent fifteen 20ft containers and one 40ft container with around 24 tonnes of donated tools. All the tools were inspected, refurbished and sorted into trade kits.

1) TOOLS WITH A MISSION (TWAM) has many opportunities for volunteering, from helping to refurbish tools to doing admin and being a volunteer speaker. Enquiries to TWAM at

2 Bailey Close, Hadleigh Road Industrial Estate, Ipswich IP2 0UD, Tel. 01473 210220. Email: post@twam.uk or Web: twam.uk. How could you be involved?

2) Close in prayer.

10. Building Begins

After all the work to successfully deliver the medical equipment to Uganda, Charles Mella then turned his attention to having plans for the clinic drawn up. He sent me a copy, together with a Bill of Quantities. The estimated total looked daunting, but 51 million Ugandan Shillings is equivalent to £11,500. I managed to find sufficient money to pay for the foundations and the first few layers of bricks to begin the walls.

I had asked Rev. Charles for his bank details and I must have spent about an hour at our bank, having all the information fed into a computer. The cashier dealing with the cash transfer called on other colleagues from time to time to give advice. Eventually she triumphantly announced, "It's been sent" and there was a feeling of euphoria amongst those who had helped. Having successfully sent one donation, future donations could be sent using the copy of the transaction as a template. Rev. Charles kept me up to date with progress on the building by sending me photos at various stages.

Progress was steady, but at times building was halted by adverse weather conditions. On one occasion Charles sent me an email saying that torrential rain had washed away lots of sand that was needed to make cement. At another time he complained that hooliganism was hampering the work. However bit by bit, the clinic began to take shape. The original clinic was doing good work in treating patients and in July 2016 Charles said that many patients were coming to the former clinic suffering from diseases like malaria, diarrhoea, cough and fever 'because it was the rainy season.' Visitors from the health authority were pleased with the new clinic.

During 2017 Charles told me the clinic was nearing completion and he wanted me to travel to Uganda for the official opening before the end of the year. I had to let him know that this was not possible because I had many commitments in the UK. I said I would plan to visit Uganda in the spring of 2018, with March as the preferred month.

1) How did you feel when something you were planning took a long time to achieve? Was there a time when a project failed to be completed?
2) Spend time thanking God for what He did through you, or seek Him for an answer to why a project didn't take place. Close in prayer.

11. Flying Solo

There are a number of people in the Stowmarket area who visit Uganda and/or Rwanda fairly frequently, including Don Egan from RSVP and Mike and Hazel Smith and Dick and Alison Fenning from New Life Fellowship. However, no one was planning a visit in March 2018. Mike said he had been to Africa every year for the past six years and he thought he would give it a miss in 2018! Mike was very helpful in giving advice about travel, food and medicines and cultural matters. And so it was in February 2018 I realised I would be travelling to Africa on my own, spending a week in Uganda and another week in Rwanda. It had to be a real step of faith.

Stowhealth have a dedicated travel nurse to advise on all matters of travel and to give injections as required. She wanted to know all the details of my trip, where I would be staying and she gave me advice on the things I should and should not do. At the end of my appointment she said she was somewhat concerned about the fact that I would be travelling alone bearing in mind my age. I was seventy-five at the time. The nurse gave me three vaccinations, for Hepatitis A, Typhoid, and Tetanus, Diphtheria and Polio as a single injection.

Stowhealth do not give Yellow Fever injections. These are administered by the Health Centre in Needham Market. When I rang, the receptionist said there were a lot of people booked in to have Yellow Fever vaccinations. When she found out I was travelling on 18th March she said, "There is no time to fit you in before you leave!" She recommended that I should go to a private clinic called Masta in the centre of Ipswich.

At Masta I was once again asked by the nurse lots of questions about what I would be doing and where I would be staying. She also gave me advice on what I should and shouldn't eat and emphasised that I should avoid all contact with dogs. She explained that the yellow fever injection had to go into the fat tissue in my arm rather than the muscle. I thought that would mean it would probably hurt, but I hardly felt it at all! The nurse said she was concerned about the fact that I would be travelling on my own and I was getting on in years. I was given an orange card stating that I had received a Yellow Fever vaccination. This is valid for life. Entry to several African countries, including Rwanda and Uganda, is refused if you have no Yellow Fever card.

My wife and two daughters were not in favour of me going to Africa on my own and then two nurses showed concern. I felt God was calling me to go and I would be working amongst Christians and I put my faith in Him.

Pauline and I had been sponsoring a child called Lilian in Rwanda since 2008 through RSVP. I contacted the office in Rwanda to see if it would be possible for Lilian and me to meet up. It seemed likely that this could be arranged.

1) What warnings have you received from family and friends that you shouldn't go on a journey or take on a particular project? How did things work out?
2) Where was God in the situation? Was prayer involved in resolving the issue?

A lot of families have a cow tethered on their land

Ploughing using oxen

Family photo

Derek and Rev. Charles waiting to leave for Entebbe

The car runs out of fuel

Apollo returns with fuel

Jane and Derek wait in a taxi until every seat is filled

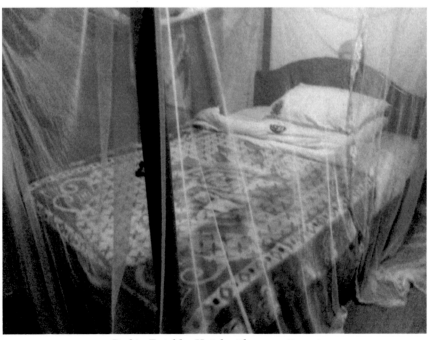

Bed in Entebbe Hotel with mosquito net

Derek outside Kigali Genocide Memorial

Jay-Jay outside Kigali Genocide Memorial

Derek with Kigali in the background

Front of the Nobleza Hotel in Kigali taken from the hotel

Derek with Lilian, Divine, mum and Cynthia in Lilian's house

Lilian and Derek

Apollo who doesn't appear in many photos because he took them

Derek signing the High School visitors book

The Diary of Derek Ames on his trip to Uganda and Rwanda

Saturday 17th March 2018

The ladies at St. John the Baptist Church, Onehouse, arranged to hold an Irish Evening on Saturday 17th March, St. Patrick's Day. Those who attended were asked to be in Trinity Hall at 6pm for a 6.30pm start. When Pauline left to attend this function, I went to bed and set my alarm for 12 midnight. Mike, a former student of mine who now runs a taxi business, said he would pick me up at 1.40am to enable me to get to Heathrow Airport in plenty of time to catch a 0650 plane to Brussels.

Sunday 18th March 2018

When I opened the curtains at midnight everywhere was covered by three or four inches of snow. Mike arrived at 01.30 and having put my luggage in the boot, he reversed down the drive. He then put his foot firmly on the accelerator of his automatic and the car zigzagged along the road, which resembled a toboggan run. He made some comment about taking it more slowly. It continued to snow more gently, but by the time we reached the A14, A11 and M11, the roads were just wet. It snowed harder as we passed Stansted Airport and as we approached Heathrow, so that as Mike dropped me off at Terminal Two, there was as much snow there as at home.

Check-in was fine and when the passengers were on the Brussels Airlines plane, technicians had to remove snow and ice from it, which made us late leaving Heathrow and then from Brussels. I was intrigued as we flew over the Sahara Desert to see the River Nile snaking into the distance. We stopped at Bujumbura, the capital of Burundi, for over an hour and several passengers left and others joined the plane. The man who came and sat next to me was flying to Entebbe and catching a plane to New York. There he would join his father in doing research on the Zika virus.

Monday 19th March 2018

As we descended to Entebbe, lightning was flickering around the airport. Instead of arriving at 22.55 on 18th March we arrived during the early minutes of the next day. It seemed to take forever to go through customs and border control, where I filled in an application for a visa costing $50. I had been told to take American dollars as these are popular at the border. As we continued to queue I wondered who would meet me and how I would recognise them. I needn't have been concerned! Most of Charles' family were there to meet me and they had made a sign saying DEREK AMES on some cardboard they had found. Their welcome was exuberant and made me feel at ease.

We had to stand under cover for a while until the torrential rain got lighter. We then went to a hotel in Entebbe where one of Rev. Charles' daughters works. She either paid the room for me or got it at a cheap rate. We talked excitedly into the early hours. Then I sank into my bed, giving God thanks for my safe journeys from Onehouse to Entebbe.

I woke at 0755, much later than usual. When unpacking my shoulder bag I realised I had lost my mobile somewhere on the two flights. I found my way to the dining area and had a breakfast of fish, roast potatoes and beans in sauce. At around the middle of the day Charles, his two sons Apollo and Mella, his daughter Jane, and her husband Richard as driver, set off for Mbale. I was given the front seat beside Richard. There was very heavy traffic around Kampala and this slowed us down, so the journey took five hours. Outside the cities the roads are very straight and most cars and vans travel very fast. There are also very large slow-moving lorries carrying a variety of agricultural crops such as bananas. We stopped to do some shopping before we reached Mbale. It was dark when we went along the road from Tororo to Mbale and vehicles continued to travel at high speed. There were also cyclists, motorcyclists and pedestrians using the road and it was raining and this mix seemed to be a recipe for disaster, but we didn't see any accidents. We enjoyed a meal of chicken, chipati, rice and matoke (mashed bananas). We continued to talk until well after midnight.

Tuesday 20th March 2018

I awoke around 0600, my usual time. After I had showered and had my quiet time, people started to arrive. This was the day Charles had chosen for the official opening of the Grace Memorial Day Care Clinic and he had invited some important guests. The first two men to arrive were part of the Retired Clergy group. Charles encouraged me to do some Bible study with them. I read Mark 1:21-28. I had only just started speaking about the passage when Jane came in to say that breakfast was ready. Afterwards we returned to the sitting room, but there was little time to continue the Bible Study. Even by the end of the day I had done no more on this passage of Scripture!

Rev. Charles was excited to welcome visitors to the Clinic. There were speeches and replies to speeches. I was given the honour of being the first to sign the Visitors Book. "Write large and write plenty and sign it large," Charles said. There were guided tours of the clinic and old and new friends to meet and conversations to enjoy with them. I met Rev. Arphaxad Namonyo again, twenty years after our first meeting, when he was Archdeacon here. He came to England to do a job swap with a Rector in Sheffield and spent a weekend with us in our Benefice in November 1998. With Arphaxad came the new Archdeacon. I also met Doctor Stephen, who had offered his services to the Clinic, as he was shortly to retire from being a GP. The Clinic stood proud with its wonderful blue roof. Inside there was a Female Ward and a Male Ward, with four beds in each, made up and waiting to welcome their first patients. These were the very beds I had watched being loaded into a container at TWAM's headquarters in Ipswich on 12th June 2012! Charles told me about a problem that had arisen when some of the first nurses to show interest in working in the Clinic came to visit. These were not local ladies and there was no accommodation in the area. Charles said, "We need to build somewhere for the nurses to stay and we need more storage space." The foundations for these are already being built.

At sometime during the day a friend of Charles got a white Volkswagen Scirocco out of the garage and checked it over. When he started it, it purred away like a well-fed cat.

As the light began to fade and thunder began to rumble around the hills, people made their way home. There is a marvellous photograph of Rev. Charles, who after kicking off his flip-flops, is sitting on a bench, perhaps reminiscing and perhaps praying about the day that was now closing.

As we went into Charles' house I realised I hadn't taken my anti-malaria tablets and I couldn't remember where I had left them. After some of us searched, Jane found the polythene bag with all my tablets in. My torch also came to light! I took all the tablets I should have taken earlier.

I took some Imodium Instants to settle my stomach and then a dose of Dioralyte, to hopefully see me through the night.

Wednesday 21st March 2018

More Diarrhoea, more Dioralyte!

Charles told me some of the family would be taking me to the border between Uganda and Kenya today. We set off early and stopped to have a look at a lovely little church where Rev. Charles used to serve as a priest. At Lwakhakha we called in to see Doctor Stephen and his wife. He then accompanied us to the border. I had to have my passport checked at the Ugandan and Kenyan Customs buildings. Doctor Stephen lives in Uganda, but has patients from both countries. Because of the uneven surfaces on which we walked, Charles and Jane were always ready to hold my hand to stop me tripping over. We said goodbye to the Doctor and travelled back to Mbale via Bumbo Secondary school, where Jane attended as a pupil and Charles was Chairman of the Board for twenty years. The Head gave us a guided tour of the school and was pleased to know that I was a former teacher. I did the customary signing of the Visitors Book. Once back at Charles' house, I asked Jane about walking to school. She used to leave home at 0730 and would meet up with others on the way, to arrive by 0830. After school Jane and her friends would leave at 1530 and Jane would arrive home at 1630.

In 2017 I developed a sore left shoulder. Treatment by a chiropractor eased the pain, but it continued to be uncomfortable. Just as the pain had almost gone, the right shoulder started aching. The pain was worse than that in the left shoulder had been and although manipulation by the chiropractor made it better, it was still sore when I left for Uganda. Imagine my surprise on the second day I was there, that when I moved my right arm, there was no pain at all. Could it have been because of the higher temperatures than in the UK? Or did someone pray for the healing of my arm? Not that I was aware of. I felt a bit like the man born blind who was healed by Jesus, but unable to explain how the healing took place. "One thing I do know: I was blind, and now I see," said the man. In my case my right shoulder had been sore for many months, but now it was completely healed and has been ever since!

During Wednesday there were suggestions about me travelling back to Entebbe on Thursday, so I would be there in good time to catch my plane to Rwanda on Saturday afternoon. Therefore that night there were presentations of a dress for Pauline and a tunic for me, together with a set of cow horns mounted with the Ugandan flag. The Presentations were accompanied by speeches thanking me for travelling to Uganda, to which I replied.

Thursday 22nd March 2018

I got packed up early, so I was ready to go as soon as farewells were said and photos were taken. Once again Apollo took some great photos. Lots of people came to say "Goodbye" and to be included in the photos. At one point a lovely young nurse walked all the way from the Clinic and putting her hand in mine said, "Thank you for coming," and disappeared as quickly as she came. This was a real tear-jerking moment.

Then off we went, with me in the front! We stopped for Jane to take something to her house. Soon after setting off the car stopped because it had run out of fuel. The car was stuck on the side of the road for an hour and then Apollo arrived by motorbike clutching a plastic jerry can and poured fuel into the tank.

We set off towards Tororo on badly rutted roads and when we came to a right-hand bend a motorcyclist coming the other way went straight into the front of the Scirocco with a loud bang, breaking the windscreen, which stayed intact. The young motorcyclist lay injured at the front of the car. When the accident happened the only people around were four men putting in footings prior to building a house. Within ten minutes or so there were about twenty people milling around waving their arms in the air as they explained what happened and why it happened. At some point someone put a bench under a tree and encouraged me to sit on it. Although it was a

shock when the accident took place, I wasn't in shock
and nor was anyone else in the car as far as I was aware.
At one point a lady in a bright yellow dress came and
gave me a big hug and introduced herself as Jane's Aunt
Mary (Grace Mella's sister). She said she had a friend
who would take us to Tororo. Jane and I set off soon
after. It was suggested the young man should go to
hospital, against his wishes. Nobody else could leave
until the police had arrived and made a report on the
accident.

We continued our journey on badly rutted roads and
eventually reached the place in Tororo where taxis leave
for Kampala. Each taxi can take fourteen passengers and
it won't leave until fourteen are on board, which in our
case took an hour to achieve! The trip was scary along
straight roads with very fast drivers and the occasional
enormous slow lorry. We reached the outskirts of
Kampala at 1730 and had to endure congestion all the
way to the taxi park in the centre of the city. This park is
amazing, having hundreds of taxis parked at all sorts of
angles on unlevel ground and yet everyone knows where
to find the right taxi. Jane found the taxi for Entebbe and
we left after six o'clock and arrived at 1900 as it was
getting dark. I had a meal in the dining room of the hotel
before going to bed and giving thanks for God's
protection throughout the day.

As a postscript to the story of the accident, Charles' son
Mella sent me an email, to my home address, hoping I

wasn't hurt as a result of the car accident. Pauline read it and asked herself, what accident?

Friday 23rd March 2018

I woke not feeling too good, so took some Dioralyte. I only have two sachets left, so Jane took me shopping in Entebbe to buy some more. I took some time looking for tee shirts for grandsons. I also shopped for items for my lunch. That night I had a meal in the hotel with Jane, Apollo and Mella, which I paid for.

Saturday 24th March 2018

I was up early and packed after breakfast. There was a misunderstanding about how I was travelling to the airport and we eventually had to get a taxi. There were long queues leading into the airport and I had to leave Apollo and Jane in a rush in order to check in on time. The plane was late in taking off, but the flight was very good, 1515-1515 (one hour flight).

When I arrived at Kigali Airport I found it difficult to convince the man doing my visa of who I was without having details of the hotel where I would be staying and without having Fred's telephone number. I bluffed my way through and met up with Fred and Jay-Jay outside Kigali Airport. I got taken to the Hotel Nobleza, where I would be staying, and I just had enough time for a quick wash before going to the New Life Church in Kigali.

Throughout the week there had been a Crusade with visiting evangelists. Saturday and Sunday were the last two days of the Crusade.

Sunday 25th March 2018

After having a shower and my quiet time, I walked over to the dining room to have a light breakfast of bread, chocolate bread, melon and mango plus African tea. The hotel had good security. On entry, everyone had to put bags and cases through an X-ray machine and walk through another X-ray machine. The men and women security guards were very friendly and got used to me coming and going.

Jay-Jay was brought to the hotel to pick me up by a driver. Worship at New Life Church was led by a band consisting of two vocalists playing guitars, a keyboard player, a drummer and a ladies and men's chorus. It was lively and loud and appreciated by the congregation. I had the opportunity to bring greetings from Christians in and around Stowmarket. Lunch for the church leaders consisted of melon, mango, spaghetti bolognaise, rice and green cabbage, prepared by the ladies. Lunch was an opportunity to chill out and chat to some of those there.

From 1500 a service of Praise and Worship began, followed by a testimony and sermon. There was a full house, as one might expect for the last service of a Crusade. Jay-Jay suggested we might leave as the appeal was being given. I was finding it difficult to stay awake by this time! I hadn't had anything to eat since lunch. Fortunately bottles of water were provided.

When I arrived back at the hotel, there was the sound of an alarm going off on my corridor and I reported this. As I went into the bathroom I noticed the floor had water on it, because of a leak behind the sink. This I reported at Reception and I was told it would be repaired the next day.

I had been impressed by the exuberant worship at New Life Church. I decided to make the services I take livelier when I got back home, by using more hymns as a foundation for the prayers and sermon. My first service was at Stowmarket Methodist Church and I chose ten hymns spread over two hymn boards! I selected lively hymns, both old and modern. Some people said ten hymns were too many, but most people appreciated the chance to have much longer periods of singing. I have continued this trend over the past eighteen months with six hymns as the norm for most services and sometimes more!

Monday 26th March 2018

I knew when I travelled to Rwanda I would find some parts of the trip very challenging. Don and Kerry visited Rwanda the year after the Genocide and they told stories of visits to genocide sites where there were heaps of bodies lying just where they had fallen. Rwandans are keen to give overseas visitors an experience of the Genocide, by visiting the Kigali Genocide Memorial and at least one of the Genocide sites. This does give answers to the question, why did the genocide happen? There is also an emphasis on what has been done since 1994 to help bring reconciliation between the Tutsis and the Hutus.

Today Jay-Jay and I travelled to the Kigali Genocide Memorial, so I could have time to read about the Genocide and how it developed across Rwanda. In just one hundred days an estimated 800,000 Tutsis and moderate Hutus were massacred by Hutu extremists. There is lots of information available about what has been done to bring lasting peace and reconciliation to Rwanda.

There are other rooms given over to other Genocides that have taken place in history, such as the Jewish Holocaust, and the Genocide led by Pol Pot and the Khmer Rouge in Cambodia. At the end of my visit I had a sick feeling inside, asking the rhetorical question 'how could human beings carry out such evil deeds?'

Jay-Jay and I then went to Kigali Airport, so I could withdraw some money from an ATM. We then had lunch in the city centre. After this I had time off at the hotel.

Tuesday 27th March 2018

I woke up in the early hours of the morning feeling off colour. I took some Dioralyte and when I got up some hours later I felt OK. After breakfast I went with Jay-Jay to a Prayer Meeting at New Life Church at 0800. The worship and prayer were excellent.

After this I was told about the Child Sponsorship Programme. There are a total of 9,407 children who have sponsors in the UK and USA. I watched a roomful of children writing letters to their sponsors, under the supervision of a member of staff from Africa New Life Ministries. I also saw girls learning hairdressing, others doing sewing and dressmaking and yet others on a personal development course. These vocational courses will equip students to move into the world of work when they leave secondary school.

Wednesday 28th March 2018

I had a good night's sleep! It was raining most of the morning. I was picked up from the Nobleza Hotel at the appointed time of 0900, by a man known as Bishop Deo, but he should have picked up someone else! He took me to a primary school, but when I arrived I was told I should have gone to a New Life Church. Bishop Deo then took me to the church. There I was told all about the sponsorship programme in that place.

When we set off again, the Toyota was slip-sliding in the mud on the roads. We visited a secondary school that should take pupils in January 2019.

At a primary school we visited, there were no pupils. On the Wednesday before Easter the pupils are given the day off, so the teachers can write their reports. Then on Thursday the children receive their reports and celebrate the end of term. Judging by how far some of the children had walked from their school, they must have been released quite early in the day! This school has 863 pupils and is the best primary school in the district.

When we were ready to leave, the car wouldn't start. The driver spent some time under the bonnet and after a few minutes it started. I must admit to being somewhat pessimistic that under the atrocious weather conditions, we might get stuck fast in the mud, but somehow we managed to get through.

Jay-Jay had asked me earlier if I would like to visit a Genocide site and when I said I would, the driver stopped off at a Roman Catholic Church on the way back to the hotel. The heavy rain and grey sky added to the solemnity of the place. The church was filled with the clothes of those who had been killed, in the places where they had been murdered. The bodies had been removed and placed in coffins piled one upon another in the basement. Now after twenty-four years, only bones remained and some of the arm and leg bones could be seen protruding from the coffins. In another part of the basement there were glass-fronted cabinets full of skulls, most of which had a slit in the top. The spirit of death was everywhere. You could feel it and almost touch it. Was there any plausible reason for such terrible slaughter? Forty-five thousand souls were destroyed in this one site. Please Lord, never let it happen again.

Thursday 29th March 2018

At breakfast Ken Bridges, an American evangelist, came and introduced himself. He said, "You know that yesterday you got into the wrong car from the hotel; that car was meant for me!" We had a good laugh about what happened and we swapped stories about how we had to take more journeys to get us to our correct destinations.

After I had put in my request to meet up with Lilian Mutesi, our sponsored child, wheels were set in motion for me to meet her at a secondary school, which is nearer to Kigali than the one she attends. Even so, it took us two hours to travel there and two hours to get back. The secondary school Lilian attends is too far from her home for her to travel to school each day, so she is a boarder.

By the time we arrived, most of the students had left. Jay-Jay took me on a walk around the school and then we had lunch with the staff in the Staff Dining Room. We continued our walk around the school and came across a girl sitting on a wall. Jay-Jay asked her name and she replied, "Lilian Mutesi." Jay-Jay said, "We have found the one we are looking for." Being British, I walked towards her with my hand outstretched, but Lilian gave me a big hug! She was a smart, pleasant-looking girl with a great smile.

Then we picked up a bag of maize meal, a bag of rice and a can of oil to take to her house. There we met her Mum, Vestine and Lilian's sisters, Devine and Cynthia. Jay-Jay commented to me that the house was a poor person's house. It only had two rooms. It was made of sticks with mud on. Jay-Jay and I shared taking photos on my ipad and we handed over the food before we departed. After a long time anticipating our meeting up, it was over in a flash.

We left for Kigali on a fast road and I was dropped back at the Nobleza Hotel. I had some toast with honey and a cappuccino at night. I watched a Premier League football match on television. I was horrified to see the number of betting adverts displayed around the pitch.

Friday 30th March 2018

I woke up at the usual time, feeling somewhat ill from diarrhoea. I took some Dioralyte and later I took some more. I took another sachet before going out shopping for biscuits and crisps. An indication that I was feeling better during the afternoon was that I was able to eat some crisps, without feeling any ill-effects. It was hot in

Kigali today with a temperature of 33 degrees C. In the evening I packed my bags and went to bed early.

I sent Pauline an email from my ipad to hers, saying that I intended being home for lunch on Easter Sunday.

Saturday 31st March 2018

I woke up in the early hours of the morning and did my final packing. I was ready in Reception before 0600 and I was picked up by a driver and Jay-Jay. Everyone who was going to fly had to get out of their car some distance from Kigali Airport and put their cases on a table. Eventually we were told to pick up our cases again. As far as I could see, the cases were not examined, so it was a pointless exercise.

Jay-Jay said I hadn't paid anything for the two days of car hire and for the food given to Lilian's family. He said I still owed eighty thousand Rwanda francs (about seventy pounds). I took my body belt off and started to count out the money. "Give it to me," Jay-Jay said. He emptied it of all the Rwanda francs and gave me back an empty body belt!

I flew from Kigali to Entebbe at 0850 and then I had the rest of the day at Entebbe until my 2325 flight to Brussels. Check-in presented no problems and there was a quick passage through passport control. While I was waiting, I noticed there was a Rwandair flight direct from Kigali to Heathrow. Had I known that, I could have avoided a day's wait at Entebbe. It was something to bear in mind if I travel to Rwanda again.

Before leaving Kigali Airport I was told I had to pick up my suitcase from the Baggage Reclaim at Entebbe Airport. This I did and had to take it with me for the rest of the day.

It was a pleasant one hour flight from Kigali (depart 0850) to Entebbe (arrive 1050). There were two young ladies working in the Immigration Office. Here my passport was signed and I was asked to pay twenty dollars for a visa. I pointed out that my visa issued on 19th March 2018 was for three months until 19th June 2018, so I did not have to pay. The ladies gave each other a crestfallen glance!

I stood outside Arrivals at Entebbe Airport and I kept getting pestered by a taxi driver to take a cab. Jane arrived after about half an hour and I was so pleased to see her. She had a driver with her and he took me to small compound of houses. A neighbour made me a Chinese curried soup, which was quite spicy. She then gave me a Chinese rice dish with peas and chicken pieces. Jane then suggested I should lie down and rest and I did so for about two hours.

As the day wore on, I was getting more and more concerned about how I was going to get to the airport. It got dark around seven o'clock and I went and spoke to a neighbour about getting to Entebbe Airport. He said I should not worry; someone would take me! He had more faith than me!

Around 2100 Jane returned and said a lift might be with Apollo or Mella, but they had no car or money. Eventually a car arrived driven by a neighbour, with Apollo and Mella inside. Jane also came with me to the airport. We stopped before the airport and four of us got out. I thanked the driver for his kindness. I had final farewells with Apollo, Mella and Jane outside the airport building.

Inside I checked in for Brussels and there was a long wait in the departure lounge. During this time an insect tried to bite me, but I killed it. It looked very much like a mosquito, but I was unsure of the type. The flight took off more or less on time at 23.25.

Sunday 1st April 2018

I dropped off to sleep soon after take-off and I was woken up when the food was brought round. I had a fish dish which didn't seem to agree with me. Later on I had other eats and drinks on the plane and I felt much better. When we landed at Brussels Airport it seemed to be too large and chaotic. I went through the duty free shop at least twice and eventually on to Gate B.

I did wonder if I would need to reclaim my case in Brussels, but it was not in Baggage Reclaim. I queued for sometime at Lost Luggage, while two other passengers managed to trace their cases. The man behind the desk looked at my papers and said he was sure my suitcase was in Brussels. I'm pleased to say he was right and I claimed it at Baggage Reclaim at London Heathrow.

At one point there were five airport staff talking to each other, while other queues of passengers were being ignored and wanted to go to their departure gate!

I had my passport checked by one lady, who sent me on to another lady who checked it. I commented that another lady had already checked it and the second lady just shrugged her shoulders!

Once on the plane I had the opportunity to look out of the window. There was obvious concern about the refuelling push down/pull up lever. Several different people, possibly as many as six, came and inspected it and gesticulated about the lever. The only outcome was for them to shrug their shoulders and walk away!

As soon as we took off we were into mist and low cloud, but we soon climbed above this. We travelled over the North Sea in blue sky and above thick cloud. We were told it would be a quick flight and after forty minutes we touched down. When the plane came to a rest, the push down/pull up lever popped up.

After going through customs and passport control, I emerged to find Mike, the taxi driver, waiting for me in arrivals. We had a good journey back and I arrived home at three minutes before one o'clock, in time for Easter Lunch!

Tailpiece

As I journeyed through Uganda and Rwanda I could sense God's presence with me, in spite of the problems and challenges along the way. The whole endeavour was a test of my faith. There was nothing I could do, except to keep moving forward.

During the time I was in Africa I knew I would have to write a book about my experiences and I knew the title would have to be "Faith That Moves Mountains".

I also realised that a week in Uganda and a week in Rwanda could not be considered in isolation from all that had happened previously in my life. I could not write about everything, but I had to describe some of the events, the Christian experiences, that had taken place in my life prior to positioning me on the cusp of this adventure. I was not able to boast and say, "Didn't I do well!" It was more a case of God taking the initiative to guide, direct and protect me during every part of my trip. To Him be the glory.

I also came to appreciate that it wasn't just me who had faith. It was dozens, no hundreds and thousands of people who had been involved in this project. Some had played major parts and others supporting roles to achieve a miracle. I am grateful to all those who were involved. I ask God to bless them.

Jesus said, *"I assure you that if you have faith as big as a mustard seed, you can say to this hill, 'Go from here to there!' and it will go. You could do anything!"* Matthew 17: 20

St. Paul wrote, *"I may have the gift of inspired preaching; I may have all knowledge and understand all secrets; I may have the faith to move mountains, but if I have no love, I am nothing."* 1 Corinthians 13:2

What about you, the reader, particularly if you have never experienced faith like this? Take God at His word and grow in relationship with Him and go where He leads. He will never let you down.

Someone has said it is easier to see God at work in our lives when we look back, but faith is going into the future with Him, confident that He will never let us down.